I AM A STAR
Child of the Holocaust

I AM A STAR

Only "special" children wear a star,
I am noticed from near and far.
They have placed a mark over my heart,
I'll wear it proudly from the start.

A star's a reward, so I've been told,
This custom passed on from days of old.
I know all that the star is revealing,
But, I'll try to have a better feeling.
                                    I am a star!

Papa told me to avoid trouble,
Come home from school on the double.
To me the star's yellow is gold,
I'll try not to act so bold.

I stand tall and proud,
My voice shouts in silence loud:
"I am a real person still,
No one can break my spirit or will!"
                                    I am a star!

I AM A STAR

Child
of the Holocaust

INGE AUERBACHER

WITH ILLUSTRATIONS BY
ISRAEL BERNBAUM

Prentice-Hall Books for Young Readers
A DIVISION OF SIMON & SCHUSTER, INC.
New York

Copyright © 1986 by Inge Auerbacher
Illustrations copyright © 1986 by Israel Bernbaum

10 9 8 7 6 5 4 3 2 1

10 9 8 7 6 5 4 3   pbk

Prentice-Hall Books for Young Readers is a trademark of Simon & Schuster, Inc.
Manufactured in the United States of America

Design by G. Laurens

Library of Congress Cataloguing in Publication Data

Auerbacher, Inge, 1934—

I am a star—Child of the Holocaust.

Bibliography: p.
    Includes index.
    Summary: The author's reminiscences about her childhood in Germany, years of
which were spent in a Nazi concentration camp. Includes several of her original poems.
    1. Holocaust, Jewish (1939–1945)—Germany (West)—Kippenheim—Personal nar-
ratives—Juvenile literature. 2. Terezín (Czechoslovakia Concentration camp)—Juve-
nile literature. 3. Auerbacher, Inge, 1934– Juvenile literature. 4. Jews —Germany
(West)—Kippenheim—Biography—Juvenile literature. 5. Kippenheim (Germany)—
Biography—Juvenile literature. 6. Holocaust survivors—United States—Biography—
Juvenile literature. I. Bernbaum, Israel, ill. II. Title. [1. Auerbacher, Inge, 1934 —   2.
Jews—Germany—Biography. 3. Holocaust, Jewish (1939–1945)—Germany (West)—
Kippenheim—Personal narratives. 4. Terezín (Czechoslovakia: Concentration camp)
5. Concentration camps—Czechoslovakia]
D810.J4A94 1986   940.53′15′0392404346   86-16410

ISBN 0-13-448458-4
ISBN 0-13-448192-5 pbk

I dedicate this book to

My parents, the guardian angels, who in the presence of great odds tried to shelter me from the blows, ease my pain, and still my hunger and fears.

Ruth and Tommy and the more than one and a half million Jewish children of the Holocaust, who now are stars of the night.

All the children of the universe, who are the new stars that shine brightly today and illuminate the world with their love.

CONTENTS

CHAPTER 1

✡

Beginnings

I remember as a little girl waiting impatiently for my birthday to arrive. My childhood birthdays were always very happy and special. That is, until my eighth birthday. I was seven years old in 1942 when I was sent with my parents to a concentration camp in Czechoslovakia. My next three birthdays marked the years of a nightmare.

Of fifteen thousand children imprisoned in the Terezin concentration camp in Czechoslovakia between 1941 and 1945, about one hundred survived. I am one of them. At least one and a half million children were killed in the Nazi Holocaust. The reason most of those children died is that they were Jewish.

Why should one remember these dreadful events? The death of one innocent child is a catastrophe; the loss of such numbers is unimaginable. Their silent voices must be heard today. This is why I feel compelled to trace the historical events that made this great evil possible and to tell my own story.

1

The fortress walls of Quebec City.

The fortress walls at Terezin.

BEGINNINGS

My hometown—Kippenheim.

Many years have passed since these events. Sometimes particular things such as a uniform, high black boots, or the sound of a whistle and train, shock me into the past. On a vacation in Quebec City, Canada, the sight of the old fortification brought the memories flooding back. The high red brick walls seemed to close in on me. I felt frightened. It was as if I were back there in Czechoslovakia. Yesterday became today. This was not Quebec City anymore; it became Terezin. It brought back to me the time when the nightmare began.

I was born on December 31, 1934, in Kippenheim, a village in southern Germany. Kippenheim is situated at the foot of the Black Forest, close to the borders of France and Switzerland. The population of around two thousand was composed of about sixty Jewish families and approximately four hundred and fifty Catholic and Protestant families. My family belonged to the middle class. Papa had his own textile business. Jews had lived in Kippenheim for at least two hundred years. I was the last Jewish child born

3

The synagogue in Kippenheim before its destruction.

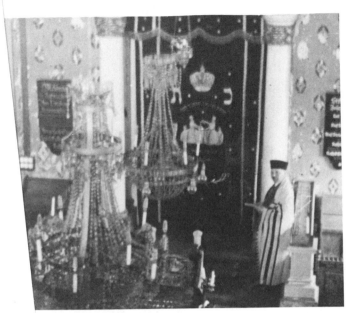

...agogue with cantor Schwab.

...gue was the center of our lives. I remember well
...r beautiful synagogue. The bright chandeliers
...eye. It was very strange and special for me to
...vab chant our Hebrew prayers. Most of the
...Kippenheim attended the Sabbath service on
...There was always a special festive spirit during
...the worshipers came dressed in their best
...mon practice to visit one another after the
...nd to invite a stranger into one's home for

...was a very strong bond among the Jewish people of
...penheim. We felt as if we were all members of an extended
family. Many of the Christians of Kippenheim were farmers, while
the Jews owned small shops and sold textiles or cattle. We were
a friendly community, and both Christians and Jews assumed
responsibility for their German citizenship, in peace and in war.

Papa was a soldier in the German army in World War I. He was only eighteen years old when an enemy bullet tore through his right shoulder and wounded him badly. He was decorated with the Iron Cross for his bravery in the service of his country.

I was the only child of Berthold and Regina Auerbacher. Papa's family had settled in Kippenheim some two hundred years earlier.

Papa as a German soldier in World War I.

Inge, grandparents and parents in Kippenheim, 1938.

Our house in Kippenheim (middle).

Most of his family made their living by buying and selling cattle, an occupation practiced by many Jews in southern Germany. Papa's grandfather bought the large house in which Papa and I were born. Many Auerbachers lived in Kippenheim, and all of us were related. Mama was born in Jebenhausen, an even smaller village some two hundred miles away. Her father was also a cattle dealer. Papa's parents had died a few years before his marriage to Mama. Three of Papa's married sisters lived in different parts of

I AM A STAR

NOVEMBER 9, 1938

It was a cold morning in November,
A day that I will always remember.
We were awakened from a peaceful sleep,
The flames of terror had begun to leap.
"Open the door, police, let us in;
Don't run or hide, you cannot win!"
We had avoided the truth and closed our eyes,
The knock on our door had caught us by surprise.
"All Jewish men are now under arrest,
Report to City Hall and join the rest!"
Grandpa attended services each day,
Now, from his prayers he was torn away.
The train rolled on toward incarceration,
Dachau, barrack number sixteen, their destination.
ARBEIT MACHT FREI* was their only greeting,
To hide the reality they would be meeting.
They wore blue and white striped uniform,
Beaten and hungry they faced the storm.
In the village only women and children were left,
Followed by rampage of tremendous ruin and theft.
Our temple became the prime target of hate,
Mama saw tablets ripped from their normal state.
The Commandments lay broken on the ground,
Heralding darkness with their crushing sound.
Broken glass crashing, echoed all day,
Our house was no place for us to stay.
In our living room, a stone grazed my head,
We ran for shelter in a backyard shed.
The volcano had exploded and begun to spew,
In its path lay the destiny of every Jew.

*work means freedom

8

BEGINNINGS

Germany, and the fourth lived in France. Two sisters had two children each. They were my older cousins Hella, Werner, Heinz, and Lore. Mama's only brother was married and lived a few hours away.

Berthold Auerbach (Moses Baruch Auerbacher), a member of my family, was one of Germany's most beloved folk writers. He lived from 1812 to 1882, and his stories of the Black Forest made him world famous. Berthold Auerbach was born and lived in Nordstetten in southern Germany, which was where my family came from.

We were a happy community in Kippenheim until the sound of marching boots shattered the peace of our tranquil village. A massive riot took place on November 9, 1938. That event is called Kristallnacht, or Night of Broken Glass. It marked the beginning of terror that would continue for seven years. I was then only three years old.

CHAPTER 2

✡

The Roots of Hatred

Anti-Semitism, or hatred of the Jews, has existed throughout the history of the Jewish religion. Many people disliked Jews because they had different customs and because they refused to become Christians. During the second half of the nineteenth century, however, a new type of anti-Semitism began to emerge. Some people began to say that Jews belonged to a different race and that Jews were racially inferior to Christians.

But who are the Jews and why did they inspire such feelings? Their origins can be traced to the patriarch Abraham, the father of a Semitic tribe of shepherds and farmers, whose revolutionary belief in the existence of one supreme God became the foundation of three great religions. The history of the Jews goes back almost four thousand years to their arrival in the biblical land of Canaan that was later called Palestine and today is called Israel. The Ten Commandments given by God to Moses serve as the basis for their religion, Judaism. Today there are people who follow this religion in almost every country in the world.

The Jews arrived in Germany about sixteen hundred years ago, around A.D. 400. They came from the Mediterranean region as traders following the Roman armies. From about A.D. 1096, during the time of the Crusades, which were Christian military expeditions that set out to recover the Holy Land from the Moslems, life became very difficult for the Jews living in Germany and other parts of Central Europe. The Crusaders offered the Jews the choice of baptism or death. "To sanctify the Name of God," they slaughtered thousands of Jews who refused to betray their religion. The church branded the Jews "Christ-killers," and Jews were thought of as evil people.

During most of the Middle Ages, the only occupations open to Jews were small trade and moneylending. The church regarded moneylending as sinful and did not permit Christians to charge interest. In this way, Jews were also associated with an evil practice.

In the Middle Ages, the Jews in Germany and other parts of Europe were sometimes forced to live in a restricted part of the city called a ghetto. In some places the Jews were isolated from other people behind walls. In the ghetto the streets were narrow and dark. Many people were poor and lived in overcrowded, crumbling houses, although some people became successful merchants. Everyone in the ghetto was forced to pay high taxes. No Jew was allowed to leave the ghetto from nightfall to daybreak and on Christian holidays. A locked gate sealed them off from the outside world. Harsh penalties were enforced if Jews were found outside of the walls during the curfew.

Conditions grew even worse when the Black Death struck. History records several outbreaks of this widespread plague and there was a particular epidemic that killed thousands of people in Europe between 1348 and 1351. The terrible sickness was blamed on the Jews, whom the Christians accused of practicing black magic and of poisoning the wells from which the Christians drew their water. Many Jews were expelled and fled eastward from Germany to Poland, Lithuania, Czechoslovakia, Hungary, Rumania, and Russia, where they established thriving Jewish communities. They were always a small minority in the total population in any country, however, and were regarded as outsiders because of their different religion and customs.

For those Jews who remained in Germany, conditions finally improved. In the early 1800s they were permitted to leave the ghetto, and they were gradually accepted by some of the Christian community. During the 1870s, they became full and equal citizens under the law throughout the country. They felt part of the German family, differing from other Germans only in religion.

A large number of Germans, however, never fully accepted their Jewish fellow citizens because of their different traditions. Jews were still not permitted to reach the highest ranks in law, government, the armed forces, or the universities. At the same time, a new wave of hostility based on a racist theory emerged in many parts of Europe. People began to believe that the Jews were a separate, inferior race. Jews tried hard to become accepted by society, some of them proudly proclaiming that their religion was secondary to their nationality.

At first, in Germany as elsewhere, most people did not believe this racist anti-Semitism. This attitude changed however as Germans looked for a scapegoat after their disastrous defeat at the end of World War I in 1918. During the war both Jews and non-Jews had fought side by side and died together for their fatherland, but with Germany's spiritual and economic defeat, this period of unity and patriotism ended. Germany was forced to sign the Treaty of Versailles in 1919 and to admit that she had started the war. She had to accept the severe measures that the Allies imposed, and to drastically reduce the army. She also had to pay large amounts of money to compensate for the suffering caused during the war, and to reduce the German Empire. A new democratic government was elected and the Weimar Republic was formed.

THE ROOTS OF HATRED

The Weimar government was troubled from the start. The post-war years saw inflation, unemployment and finally, in 1929, a world depression. Jewish people were blamed for the ailing economy and extremists called for them to be pushed out of German society. Racist anti-Semitism gathered support. In this climate of hostility and depression the stage was set for Hitler's Nazi party to emerge.

CHAPTER 3

✡

Adolf Hitler's Rise to Power

Adolf Hitler was born on April 20, 1889, in Braunau, a village in Austria near the German border. He was not a gifted student, and he failed as an artist. In 1907, he moved to Vienna where his political aspirations were born. At the age of twenty-four he arrived in Munich, Germany, and soon was in the midst of World War I. He volunteered for service in the German army, fought in many battles and reached the rank of corporal.

In 1919 in Munich, Hitler joined a small nationalist group called the German Workers' Party, which changed its name a year later to the National Socialist German Workers' Party. This group later became known as the Nazi Party.

On November 8, 1923, Hitler held a rally in a Munich beer hall and called for a Nazi revolution against the Bavarian government. The following day he attempted to seize power. This event became known as the Beer Hall Putsch, which means revolution. Hitler was arrested for treason and sentenced to five years in prison. He only served nine months of his prison term. During his time in prison, he put his ideas into a book called *Mein Kampf*, or *My Struggle*.

Many Germans were enchanted by Hitler's magnetism and regarded him as their savior. He made it clear in *Mein Kampf* what he would do to create a new Germany. He intended to establish a New Order (the Third Reich) that would last a thousand years. Hitler said that Germany must rid itself of all Communists and Jews, whom he considered enemies of the state. He held a special hatred for the Jews and singled them out to bear the blame for all of Germany's troubles. Hitler believed the Jews as a race were inferior to the Aryan (German) "Master Race." Pure Aryans, he contended, were large-boned, blond, and blue-eyed, although Hitler himself was short and dark-haired. He believed that all Jews had to be eliminated because their blood was inferior to that of the German Aryans. He said Jewish blood would pollute the "master race." The truth is all blood types occur in all races and all nations. Hitler's brand of anti-Semitism would be the worst ever seen anywhere.

After Hitler was released from prison, he convinced the government that his party would respect the law. He rose steadily to power and gained support from labor unions, business, industry, and agriculture. In the New Order the swastika, or twisted cross, became the symbol of the Nazi Party.

In 1930 Hitler's brown-shirted storm troopers, or Sturmabteilung (SA), marched through the streets with the Nazi swastika flag, singing, "Today we rule Germany, tomorrow the world!"

On January 30, 1933, Hitler was appointed Chancellor of Germany by the ailing President von Hindenburg, who died eighteen months later. After von Hindenburg's death, Hitler abolished the presidency and made himself the absolute ruler, or Fuehrer, of the nation. Crowds cheered him with cries of "Heil, Hitler," which means Hail, Hitler. The Weimar Republic, which had lasted from 1918 to 1933, was over.

From the start, Hitler's government was based on lies and deception. Hitler had a secret police called the Gestapo and a special security force known as the SS, for Schutzstaffel, also called the Blackshirts. He named Josef Goebbels chief of propaganda, assigning him to spread his doctrine, but Hitler himself was an excellent speaker and influenced both young and old. Hermann Goering became second in command to Hitler. Rudolf Hess was Hitler's secretary, and Heinrich Himmler became the party's chief executioner.

Two themes dominated Hitler's dictatorship from beginning to end: *Lebensraum*, the belief that Germany needed more land and was entitled to invade her neighbors in order to get it; and *Judenfrage*, the theory that the entire Jewish race had to be eliminated. During the Hitler regime, the Nazis did their best to carry these ideas to their murderous extremes. Anti-Semitism became official government policy.

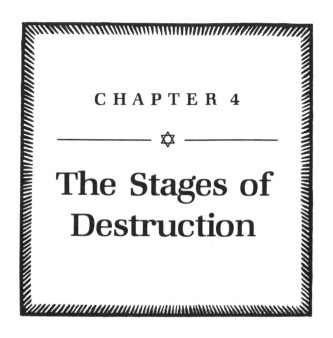

CHAPTER 4

✡

The Stages of Destruction

The first stage in Hitler's planned destruction of the Jews, from 1933 to 1938, was to deprive Jews in Germany of all rights. Decrees followed one another in rapid succession. The first decree was for a one-day boycott of Jewish shops and businesses. Then the ritual slaughter of animals in accordance with Jewish dietary laws was forbidden. There were public burnings of books written by Jews. The first German concentration camp—Dachau, located near Munich—was established in 1933.

Between 1933 and 1935 most Jewish teachers, public servants, and professionals lost their jobs. On August 2, 1934, Hitler was named president and commander-in-chief of the armed forces. The Third Reich had become a reality. On September 15, 1935, the so-called Nuremberg Laws, which were anti-Jewish racial laws, came into effect. Jews could no longer be German citizens. Those of mixed Jewish and Aryan backgrounds were called *Mischlinge*, or half-breeds, and were subjected to the same harsh laws. Jews were

I AM A STAR

no longer permitted to fly the German flag. In 1938, Germany put
its dream of world domination into action by annexing Austria. The
takeover of the Sudetenland from Czechoslovakia followed soon
afterward.

On July 6, 1938, President Franklin D. Roosevelt of the United
States of America invited people from thirty-three nations to meet

IF ONLY

They met at Evian on Geneva's shore,
Holding the key to freedom's door.
Thirty-two nations claimed open mind,
They saw the light; yet acted blind.

If only!

Talking for days; finding excuse,
Leaving us prey to mounting abuse.
In humanity's sea we were adrift,
Our doom would be violent and swift.

If only!

How many lives could have been spared,
Had one FREE nation really cared?
Human beings offered for sale,
Our cries rose up to no avail.

If only!

We still feel the pain and we weep,
This nightmare will not let us sleep.
A page in history; one must learn,
Yesterday us, tomorrow your turn?

If only, if only!

18

THE STAGES OF DESTRUCTION

at Evian, France. Thirty-two nations sent representatives to this conference to discuss how they could aid political refugees who wanted to emigrate from Germany and Austria. These refugees were mainly Jews, whose lives were becoming unbearable in those countries. The Evian Conference failed. A German newspaper ran this headline: "Jews for Sale—Who Wants Them? No One!"

On November 7, 1938, Herschel Grynszpan, a seventeen-year-old Polish Jewish student, walked into the German embassy in Paris and shot Ernst vom Rath, a minor German official. Grynszpan had been angered by the forced deportation of his parents from Germany to Poland. The Grynszpans, like many other Polish Jews, had lived in Germany for a long time without seeking citizenship and now were mercilessly thrown out of the country. Vom Rath died two days later on November 9, 1938.

This incident triggered a nationwide riot in Germany and Austria on the night of November 9, 1938. Kristallnacht, or the Night of Broken Glass, continued for two days. Almost all Jewish houses of worship were put to the torch. Jewish homes and businesses were looted and destroyed. Many Jewish men were arrested and sent to concentration camps. Those who resisted were shot.

Soon afterward, Jews were forbidden to attend German schools and to own property or businesses. The Nazi scheme was to make conditions for the Jews impossible by keeping them from making a living. This tactic, they hoped, would drive the Jews out of Germany.

Many Jews managed to leave Germany and Austria, but most of those who lived in Eastern Europe were stranded. Those Jews who remained in Germany, in spite of all humiliation, were still attached to the country they had lived in for so many years. Most of them thought this, too, would pass, not recognizing the danger they were facing. When they finally were ready to leave, they found that the doors of the outside world would not open. Escape routes were blocked because of immigration quota systems, unemployment, and general apathy in the countries of the free world.

I AM A STAR

On September 1, 1939, Germany invaded Poland. World War II had begun. Hitler, drunk with power, told his soldiers: "Close your eyes to pity! Act brutally!" His armies would conquer many countries in Europe before his defeat by the Allies in 1945. The fate of the remaining Jews in Europe was sealed. The Nazis were planning total extermination. The term Holocaust, which means complete destruction by fire, is often used when speaking of this period of slaughter and brutality.

The extermination of the Jews took place in stages. At first the Nazis resettled the Jews into ghettos and concentration camps, where many died of starvation and disease. The able-bodied were

Map of Europe showing how far Nazi power extended.

THE STAGES OF DESTRUCTION

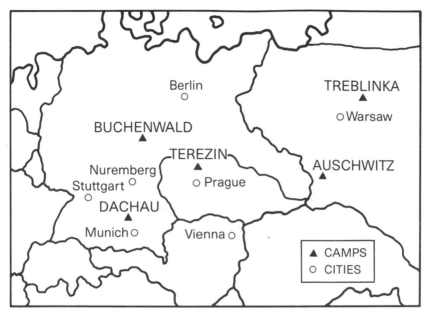

Berlin
○

TREBLINKA
▲

○ Warsaw

BUCHENWALD
▲

TEREZIN
▲

Nuremberg
○
Stuttgart ○
DACHAU
▲

○ Prague

AUSCHWITZ
▲

Munich ○   Vienna ○

▲ CAMPS
○ CITIES

Map of Europe showing the position of some of the concentration and extermination camps.

often forced to perform slave labor. The largest ghettos were in Poland, where many of Europe's Jews lived. On November 15, 1940, the Warsaw Ghetto, containing approximately 500,000 Jews, was sealed off from the outside world.

In March 1941, Adolf Eichmann was appointed head of the Gestapo section for Jewish affairs. His job was to speed up the extermination. After September 1941, all German Jews over the age of six were required to sew a large yellow Star of David on the left breast of their clothing, and were forbidden to walk in public without it.

As the Nazi hordes marched farther east, more Jews came under their control. Special death squads called Einsatzgruppen rounded up the Jews, forced them to dig their own graves, and then shot them. By the beginning of 1942, these squads had killed close to 1.4 million people.

Prisoners arrive at the Small Fortress at Terezin. They must pass through the gate with the inscription—"Arbeit macht Frei."

The elimination of the Jews was not going fast enough for Hitler, however. Cheaper and quicker methods of killing were needed. At the Wannsee Conference of January 20, 1942, the Nazi leaders worked on the details of the Final Solution, the plan to kill all of Europe's Jews. The concentration camps and ghettos were eventually to be liquidated. Their surviving population would be sent to extermination camps. The largest of these was Auschwitz in Poland. This camp was equipped with poison-gas chambers and crematoria, ovens in which the bodies were burned. Four million people died in Auschwitz. Most of them were Jews.

The Germans tried to hide their intention of murder. They used terms like umgesiedelt (resettled) instead of deported, and they hung signs saying "Arbeit macht Frei" (work means freedom), over the gates of the camps. When prisoners entered an extermination camp, a flick of a finger by a Nazi doctor selected an individual for a life of hard labor and starvation or for immediate death. Those who were sentenced to die were forced to enter the "showers," which actually were gas chambers. They were given a piece of soap and an SS officer told them to breathe deeply. He said it would help their lungs to stay healthy by disinfecting them and would keep them from getting sick. Within a short time only their ashes would remain.

CHAPTER 5

✡

My Story

I remember well that November day when Papa and Grandpa were sent to the Dachau concentration camp. It was Kristallnacht. Grandma and Grandpa had come to visit us in Kippenheim and were caught with us in the unforgettable terror. How thankful we were to welcome my father and grandfather home again a few weeks later. They spoke quietly about having been beaten and mistreated in that awful place, saying, "The child must not hear these things." Soon afterward, Papa lost his textile business.

It was time to leave Germany, but where could we go? Most nations of the free world were closing their doors. In May 1939, we packed our belongings and sold our house. We left our village and moved in with my grandparents in Jebenhausen. This was meant to be a short stay, since we still hoped to find a way of leaving Germany. Grandpa soon succumbed to a broken heart. He died from a combination of illness and a disappointment in the country he loved.

The village of Jebenhausen.

Inge's grandparents' house in Jebenhausen.

Grandma, Inge and Mama at Grandpa's grave in Jebenhausen, 1940.

Inge with doll Marlene and girlfriend in Jebenhausen, 1940.

Inge with her grandparents and favorite doll carriage.

Even so, some of my happiest memories of my childhood go back to the two years we spent in Jebenhausen. My grandparents were the only remaining Jewish family in this village of one thousand inhabitants. The other children were friendly and had no bad feelings toward me. I became their leader as we marched up and down the street singing the popular songs of this time, which often contained Nazi propaganda. The frenzy of the day was infectious. We did not understand the implications of these songs in our childhood innocence.

Even though there was little anti-Jewish feeling in Jebenhausen, my grandparents had always practiced religion with caution. According to the Jewish religion, the forty year period during which Moses and his flock wandered in the desert is commemorated through the Feast of the Tabernacles, or Succos. This festival calls for a symbolic hut (a succo) to be built of reeds, tree branches, and grass. The interior is decorated with colorful ornaments and the fruits, vegetables, and flowers of fall. The roof of the attic room in my grandparents' house was lifted off and the room converted into a succo. Although the room could not be seen, after my grandpa died, we did not dare to celebrate even in this secret way.

Every day new restrictive decrees were announced. Jews were compelled to give up all their gold and silver. They had to take Israel or Sara as a middle name to make them recognizable as Jews. My name became Inge Sara Auerbacher. Some of the villagers of Jebenhausen were not alarmed by these anti-Semitic laws and continued their friendship with us, even though Christians were forbidden to associate with Jews. A few of the farmers continued to give us food.

Our beloved Christian friend, Therese, who had worked as a servant in my grandparents' house for over twenty years, placed food behind my grandfather's gravestone at night for us to pick up in the morning. She was able to save a few of our things until after the war, including two family photo albums and some of our prayer books. The pictures shown in this book were among the items she kept for us. By associating with us, the people who helped us risked their lives. They were very brave.

The Jewish school at the Jewish Community Center in Stuttgart.

Jewish children were no longer permitted to attend regular schools. I had to walk two miles to Goeppingen, a larger neighboring town, and then travel one hour by train to attend classes in Stuttgart. This was the only Jewish school in the province. I needed special travel permission papers for this trip, since Jews were no longer allowed to move freely.

This trip became even more hazardous, when, on September 1, 1941, Jews were made to sew the yellow Star of David on their clothes as a distinguishing mark. On the star the word *Jude*, which means Jew in German, was written in Hebrew-like letters. Papa told me to sit in such a position on the train so as to "naturally" cover my yellow badge, even though it was strictly forbidden to hide that "mark of shame." This was not always possible, and other children taunted and heckled me. Some people took pity on me, though. One day a Christian woman left a bag of rolls next to my seat. She must have felt sorry for the little Jewish six-year-old child traveling such a long distance by herself.

The yellow Star of David with the word Jude *meaning Jew in German.*

The "Final Solution," the Nazi plan to liquidate all the Jews in Europe, began for us in 1941. Rumors of our "resettlement" were the talk of the day. Many people made frantic attempts to leave Germany, but to no avail. All borders were closed to us.

Deportations to the "East" began in late 1941. One morning, my grandmother, my parents, and I received our orders for transport. Papa was a disabled veteran of World War I and used this as a plea for us to be spared. He succeeded, but we were not able to help my grandmother. She and most of my classmates were sent to Riga, Latvia. I shall never forget our tearful good-byes as we watched her descend the stairs in the Stuttgart railroad station until she was out of view. I would never see her again. Almost all of these unfortunate people became victims of the Einsatzgruppen, in a forest near Riga. They had to dig their own graves before they were shot.

MY STORY

Children of the Jewish houses in Goeppingen, 1941. Only Inge in the striped hat would survive the war.

First page of Inge's transport orders to the concentration camp.

We were forced out of my grandparents' home in Jebenhausen and relocated in one of the "Jewish houses" in Goeppingen. My parents were sent to work for very little money in a women's undergarment factory. My school in Stuttgart was closed before I completed the first grade.

The war was in full gear in 1941. We were awakened many nights by the screaming air raid sirens, which always badly frightened me. Most of the Allied bombs at this time were dropped far from where we were living, however.

DEPORTATION

It was a morning like no other,
The deadly letter was opened by Mother.
She screamed out with a loud cry:
"It is true, we can no more deny,
We are no longer citizens with a name,
Now a transport number replaces the same."
Too long we had closed danger's door,
Hoping for life as it was before.
The document showed no cause or reason,
Mama packed up clothes for every season.
No statement of where we were going,
Rumors of shipment to a camp were growing.
We were herded to a gathering place,
For resettlement designated for our "race."
Packed together on the sealed train,
Would we ever see our home again?
We passed through an unfamiliar countryside,
Two days later loud shouts ended our ride.
We had arrived at the Bohušovice station,
"Drop everything—march—no confrontation!"
Guards surrounded us with whip and gun,
Fatigue and fear plagued everyone.
The old and infirm fell to the ground,
And pierced the air with a shrieking sound.
Two miles later Terezin was in sight,
Its high walls would soon shut out the light.
Searched and left with only one dress,
We were sent to the Dresden Fortress.
Here we bedded down on the bare floor,
Wondering what else was for us in store.
Night had come with its enveloping curtain,
Our situation was hopelessly uncertain.
We had arrived in Satan's new city,
Where was the world? There was no pity!

Inge's identification papers with the letter "J" for Jew. It is stamped on the day of deportation to concentration camp: "umgesiedelt 22.8.42" or resettled, August 22, 1942.

Waiting for food in the collection center at Killesberg in Stuttgart.

I AM A STAR

Finally, our turn to be deported came on August 22, 1942. There was no longer any way to avoid a transport. I was now number XIII-1-408, a person without any citizenship. We packed our meager belongings according to the very specific instructions we were given. All our money was taken from us. The police came to our apartment. Mama was told to place our keys on the dining room table. The official then said, "Now you can go!"

We were herded into a school gymnasium in Goeppingen and searched. My greatest fear was that the SS would take away my doll, Marlene. She had been a gift from my grandmother, the only token of remembrance I had of her. The officials removed Marlene's head to see if any valuables were hidden inside her hollow body, but they finally decided to let me keep my doll. I was not so fortunate, however, with a wooden decorative pin. An SS officer took a liking to it and tore it off my dress.

A DUTCH BOY PIN

A Dutch boy pin nestled on my dress,
Standing strong with pride and happiness.
Greedy fingers tore him from me,
Did those hands know my destiny?
My last ornament before I'd depart,
These claws ripped him off and broke my heart.

"You won't need this where you are going!"

A gift from my mother, lovingly attached,
All my struggles hopelessly outmatched.
I ponder, Whom was that pin given to?
Could another girl find joy if she knew?
Was it discarded, is it part of the past?
Does he still hope to find me at last?

The hall of the collection center for deportation at Killesberg in Stuttgart.

Arrival in Bohušovice and the march to Terezin.

From Goeppingen we were taken to Stuttgart, which was the main gathering place for Jews who were being transported. I was the youngest of almost twelve hundred people in the group. We were housed in a large hall at Killesberg which was usually used for flower shows. We bedded down for two days on the bare floor.

CHAPTER 6

✡

A Place of Darkness

Our destination was Terezin, or Theresienstadt as it was called in German, a concentration camp in Czechoslovakia about forty miles north of Prague. It was built in 1780 by Hapsburg Emperor Joseph II in memory of his mother Empress Maria Theresa. The garrison was abandoned by the military in the 1880s and was settled by civilians. By the late 1930s, Terezin was in a state of bad deterioration.

On October 10, 1941, Reinhard Heydrich, Adolf Eichmann, and other high-ranking Nazi officials selected Terezin as a transit camp for Jewish deportees before their extermination in the East. The Nazis masked the camp as a "model ghetto" for propaganda purposes. The first Jews sent there in November 1941 were from Czechoslovakia. They were followed next by the elderly from Germany and Austria who were not expected to live long anyway. Many prominent doctors and lawyers, decorated war veterans, and distinguished Jewish leaders, like Rabbi Leo Baeck from

Germany, were sent to Terezin. Their immediate deportation East to the killing centers would have aroused suspicion. Eventually, Jews from all walks of life arrived at Terezin from Austria, the Netherlands, Denmark, and other European countries, including people whose parents were of mixed Jewish and Christian origin.

I remember a particular transport of at least one thousand children from Poland in the summer of 1943. They came dressed in rags and were all very thin and dirty; many were sick. All were ordered by the SS to remain in quarantine in a special area. Rumors spread that they came from Bialystok, Poland, and had seen their parents shot before their eyes. A short time later they were sent to the gas chambers in Auschwitz.

WALLS

Walls, walls, walls are eyeing us all around,
Silently absorbing each wailing sound.
Unlike Zion's, where they are our soul,
Here even our thoughts are under control.

Walls covered by a grassy knoll,
Death-defying leapers take their toll.
The red brick demons stand very firm,
Quiet objects demanding their term.

Soldiers march on them to and fro,
Guarding people with no place to go.
These walls are closing in on me,
Dare I dream to climb them and flee?

I AM A STAR

Terezin consisted of huge brick barracks, underground cells and old broken-down houses. It was sealed off from the outside world by high walls, deep water-filled trenches, wooden fences, and barbed wire. Radio, telephone, and newspaper communication with the outside was strictly forbidden. On rare occasions, however, bits of war information leaked into the camp. These rumors were called "latrine talks," because the prisoners exchanged news in the public bathrooms. Stories often changed in content as they spread through the camp.

It was also forbidden for women to give birth, but a few hundred children were born during the years I was there. Breaking this rule usually meant immediate shipment to the East for both mother and child. Yet, miraculously a handful of these babies survived the war in Terezin.

Terezin.

A PLACE OF DARKNESS

The walls and trenches surrounding Terezin.

Backyard of the disabled veterans quarters in which we lived.

Terezin was originally built to house 7,000 people, but at times the camp was crowded with 60,000 prisoners. A Jewish Council of Elders was set up to regulate internal affairs. This group was chaired by the Judenaeltester, or chief of elders. The council's most important duty was to draw up lists of inmates for deportation to the East, following SS instructions. Terezin was under the absolute rule of a Nazi SS commandant. Between 1941 and 1945, a total of 140,000 people were sent to Terezin; 88,000 of them were shipped to the killing centers of the East; and 35,000 died of malnutrition or disease in Terezin.

Prison blocks at the Small Fortress in Terezin.

A short distance from the large fortress, where I was, across the Ohře River was a smaller fortress called Kleine Festung. This also belonged to the Terezin complex, but it was a military prison and had its own SS commandant. It also served as a place of extra punishment for any misconduct we in the large fortress might commit. Our crimes were things like stealing potatoes, or being caught drawing a picture of the "real" conditions of the camp. The small fortress had solitary confinement cells and an area for firing squads. It was a brutal place that was feared as much as being sent to the East.

A PLACE OF DARKNESS

Terezin was a gruesome place. The inhuman conditions brought out the best and worst behavior in people. Hunger makes people selfish and irritable. After our arrival at Terezin we went through the Schleuse, a body-and-belongings search area in an underground cell. After the search for valuables we were sent to the attic of the Dresden Fortress, which was a particularly large brick army barrack containing exercise courtyards and gaping archways. This is where the "Angel in Hell"—Mrs. Rinder, a Czech woman—found us lying on the bare stone floor. She asked someone whether there was a child in the newly arrived transport. Fingers pointed towards me.

AN ANGEL IN HELL

We searched the dump for each potato peeling,
Stole from the dead without guilt or feeling.
Nothing seemed to change; time stood still,
Was there anyone left with good will?

To this planet of shadow and despair,
An angel came to give help and care.
One hand was clutched by her little son,
She wanted to mother everyone.

Through time she moved on unseen wings,
Bearing food and other needed things.
This stranger reached out with heart and hands,
Asking no thanks, or making demands.

Both would never leave the abyss,
Or be touched again by life's kiss.
I search my heart for an answer, Why, why?
Where was justice, why their sentence to die?

Hundreds of people were moving hopelessly in this dark, airless, hot area. They stumbled over the covered dead bodies and got lost in the mass of new arrivals. Mrs. Rinder had arrived earlier in Terezin with her husband and young son Tommy. This good lady, whom we had never met before, gave me a mattress by dividing her son's mattress in half. Mr. Rinder was fortunate to work in one of the community kitchens and therefore was able to share some extra food with us at times. A deep friendship developed between us until the fall of 1944, when the entire Rinder family was deported to Auschwitz and death in the gas chambers.

Under these terrible conditions, some people lost the will to live and took their own lives. A few days after our arrival in Terezin, my father saw a man starting to jump from an attic opening of the Dresden Fortress. Papa managed to grab the man's legs and pull him back inside. To his amazement, it was an old man from our transport. Papa spoke encouraging words to him and made him promise not to repeat this act. The next morning a broken body lay lifeless in the fortress courtyard. Papa identified him. It was the same old man.

Sleeping quarters at Terezin.

A PLACE OF DARKNESS

Standing on line for food at Terezin.

Soon after our arrival we were moved to a different area. Most men, women, and children were housed in separate quarters. I had the good fortune to stay with my parents in the disabled war veterans' section. Life was especially harsh and strange for children. We slept on the floor or, if lucky, on straw-filled mattresses, packed like sardines on double and triple-deck bunk beds. The rooms were smelly and steamy in summer and freezing in winter. We grew up fast and became self-reliant. The most important words in our vocabulary were *bread, potatoes,* and *soup.* I used to look out from the room where some birds had made a nest high up on a ridge. How I envied them. They could fly away from all this misery, while we stayed walled in.

Three times a day we stood in line, our metal dishes in hand, to receive our daily food rations from the community kitchens.

GAMES

We were not like other children at play,
The future becoming more uncertain every day.
Our playground was a garbage heap,
And the treasures from it we'd reap.
There our curiosity was stilled,
Finding remnants from dreams unfulfilled.
We put our imagination to the test:
Who could describe a sumptuous meal best?

"Don't run around and waste your energy,
Save your shoes, don't use them foolishly!"
We played checkers on a hand-drawn board,
With black and white buttons we scored.
"What was your day's flea and bedbug catch?
Let's have a bunk bed running match."
We saw carts piled with bodies roll along,
And turned our heads away to sing a song.

A PLACE OF DARKNESS

Most of the kitchens were located in the open courtyards of the huge barracks. The lines were always very long. It was especially hard in the winter, waiting in the bitter cold. Breakfast consisted of coffee, a muddy-looking liquid, which always had a horrible taste. Lunch was a watery soup, a potato, and a small portion of turnips or so-called meat sauce; and dinner was soup. By the time the people reached the barrels from which the food was ladled out, they were so hungry and exhausted that they immediately gulped their portion down.

SOUP

Three times a day we stand on line,
Pretending that on delicacies we dine.
It spills over clothes and makes a spot,
People fight, push and shove a lot.
                    Soup, soup drink it down!

Today's dinner is water with caraway seed,
Food unacceptable even as animal feed.
I don't have a choice and gulp it down,
A little disgruntled wearing a frown.
                    Soup, soup run for seconds!

It is poured into a metal can,
Ladled out by an impatient man.
Thin or thick, with or without taste,
Not a bit of it will go to waste.
                    Soup, soup means life!

I must get more and get my fill,
To keep the cries of hunger still.
With a spoon we scrape out the last drop,
Not until barrel is empty do we stop.
                    Soup, soup, soup, soup!

I remember Mama marking off each day on our rationed loaf of bread to make certain that we would have enough left to last us a week. This was often difficult. When the hunger pains became too strong, she regretfully cut slightly into the next day's portion of bread.

Birthdays presented a special challenge. One year I received a potato cake the size of my palm, prepared from a mashed boiled potato with just a hint of sugar in it. Another year Marlene, my doll, was given a new outfit sewn from rags. On my tenth birthday my gift was a poem my mother had written especially for me.

The smell of death was everywhere. Many old people had been sent to Terezin. They could not withstand the terrible conditions and died of starvation or disease. Two-wheeled hand-drawn carts

Two—wheeled cart similar to those used for moving things in the camp.

were used alternately to transport our food and to take away the sick and the dead. We hand-pumped most of our water from polluted wells.

There were constant epidemics due to overcrowding and lack of hygiene. Rats, mice, fleas, and bedbugs were a constant menace to us. I contracted scarlet fever soon after we arrived in Terezin and spent four months in the so-called hospital. All the patients were isolated from the rest of the camp. I feared the worst—my parents' deportation to the East without me. My condition grew worse every day as more complications arose. I was not expected to live. Measles, mumps, and a double middle ear infection followed the scarlet fever in rapid succession. I was infested with worms, I lost my voice, and my body was covered with boils.

Men washing themselves in a fortress courtyard at Terezin, using water drawn from a hand-pumped well.

IN THE HOSPITAL

We are two in a bed; the paint is peeling,
Flies cover the walls from floor to the ceiling.
I share my place with a younger child,
Most of the time our bed is defiled.

We speak in different tongues; yet we are one,
Two small windows let in rays of the sun.
At least fifty share our chamber here,
There is a feeling of death stalking near.

How thin our fever-ravaged bodies have become.
I have lost my voice; my senses feel numb.
We must leave this dungeon and recuperate,
What is our future, what will be our fate?

A PLACE OF DARKNESS

I made a new friend in the hospital. Ada was of German Jewish origin. She taught me a new song about Palestine, which is now Israel. Its words spoke of a perpetual paradise where the cedars of Lebanon kiss the sky. She promised me we would soon go to this place. "Just hold on a little longer," she used to say. Ada's dream never came true. She died at the age of nine in Auschwitz.

Just before my eighth birthday I was released from the hospital. Before I joined my parents, I was washed in a large bucket containing a disinfecting solution to help remove some of my lice. My hair had been cut very short, and Mama used a small comb with narrow teeth that dug into my scalp to try to rid me of the remaining lice. I still can feel the awful stomach cramps from dysentery, and the long walk to the public toilets, which were always overcrowded and without any privacy.

Most of the adults in the camp were forced to work. Some women were selected to work as slave laborers splicing mica, a product used by the Nazis in their war effort. This was considered a good job, since it sometimes kept a person from being sent to the East. Mama's first job in the camp was washing laundry from typhus patients. One day she found a very high stack of what appeared to be soiled sheets. As she tried to gather them up, she found to her dismay that they were dead bodies covered with sheets. People died like flies in Terezin.

Mama's fortune improved when she became a nurse in the old people's hospital. Often she chose the night shift so as to get an extra ration of bread. I recall those deathly sick people holding sticks to ward off the rats, which sometimes jumped into their beds. Every night someone died, and the staff divided the leftover rations and clothes among themselves.

Papa became a scavenger, rummaging every day in the garbage dump in search of potato peelings and rotten turnips. If he was extra lucky he might find boiled horse bones that we could cook again to extract any leftover fat and grizzle.

I made a bed for my doll in a cardboard box at the head of my upper-level bunk bed. One day I discovered a dead mouse in it, another victim of starvation. Not even a mouse could find enough leftover crumbs of bread to survive.

51

DIAMONDS ON THE SNOW

Winter had come; the earth lay frozen,
To be in Terezin, we had not chosen.
Snow covered up blight with a veil,
Bad times for hardy; worse for the frail.
Mama had gotten some valuable jewels,
Endangered her life by breaking the rules.
She entered the cellars during camp's curfew,
A certain death sentence, if anyone knew.
Oh, what great wealth and secret we kept,
While on those precious diamonds we slept.
Rumors abounded of our block's inspection,
We must conceal them before their detection.
In the rubbish Papa found an old suitcase,
There wasn't one minute to waste in this race.
His ingenuity produced a master plan,
A spot under rag heap that no one would scan.
He threw them all into the cavernous box,
To keep them safe, despite broken locks.
He peered out the door—the time was right—
And ran with the treasure through the night.
One must not hestitate, be fearful, or stall,
Running on icy snow soon made him fall.
The suitcase opened, its contents all around,
Cushioned by the snow, not making a sound.
They lay like gems in a store on display,
Their contrasting hue made them easy prey.
Papa carefully picked up every one,
In a few minutes, his job would be done.
Placing the valuables in the chosen spot,
A deserted place that everyone forgot.
Nervously, we awaited Papa's quick return,
His safety our chief worry and concern.

The door opened, his mission a success,
Next day's search would bring much distress.
In a few days the coast was clear,
We would again have our valuables near.
Each and every "diamond" on the snow,
To us a treasure—a precious potato.

I WISH

I wish I were a little bird
up in the bright blue sky,
& that sings and flies just
where he will and no one
she asks him why.

I wish I could run free,
And play to my heart's desire.
Climb mountains, walk on soft grass,
Never would I tire.

I wish these strange conditions,
Were no more than a nightmare.
That there are still people somewhere,
Who understand and care.

I wish I could sleep on a soft bed,
And eat a good meal.
Never again to hunger,
To barter, and to steal.

I wish I would wake up
To a new and brighter morn.
In another time, a different land,
And be reborn.

I AM A STAR

Some attempts were made to teach us in *Beschaeftigung*, or keeping-busy classes. School was absolutely forbidden, but some heroic teachers gathered us children in attics and other places where there was a little space. They taught us from memory, since very few schoolbooks were smuggled into the camp. In an English class I learned "I Wish I Were," which I wrote into a worn notebook and hid from view on one of Eichmann's visits. It was only recently that I completed this poem with my own thoughts.

I remember vividly the Bohušovice Ravine roll call on November 11, 1943. It was the only time I ever got outside the camp walls. We were told that some inmates were missing and a complete count had to take place outside the camp. At least forty thousand of us were herded very early in the morning onto a large muddy field. It was a cold and rainy day. We did not know what was going to happen to us. Our future seemed uncertain. We were surrounded by soldiers and guns. No food was given to us the entire day. No toilets were available to us. I watched in horror as an SS man smashed the butt of his rifle into my mother's back. Some people had actually escaped and may have got away. News of our outing leaked out and was broadcast on the English radio. Consequently, direct orders from Berlin halted any further action on that day. We returned to the camp after midnight. Many people died on the field from exhaustion, cold, and severe beatings.

By the end of 1943, rumors of mass murder in the East had begun to circulate. The International Red Cross requested permission to inspect a camp to find out if these accusations were true. The Nazis chose Terezin for this purpose. Many months passed before this request was granted on June 23, 1944. In the meantime Terezin went through a "beautification" program. Certain parts of the camp were cleaned up. Some people were given new clothing and good food to eat. A few children received chocolates and sardine sandwiches just as the commission walked past them. I was not one of the lucky ones. In the center of town an orchestra played in a newly erected band shell. The areas filled with the things that had been stolen from us were carefully locked up. Blind, crippled, and sick people were warned to stay out of sight. Even the most brutal SS officer, Rudolf Haindl, acted friendly on that day. Transport lists to the East were carefully hidden. The International Red Cross inspections team left the camp believing the immense deception that Terezin was a "model" place for Jews to live in. A film was made at this time to document the "good" conditions in Terezin.

Camp money.

I AM A STAR

DECEPTION

All is readied for a Red Cross inspection,
Our very existence is based on deception.
Could the world be lulled to believe,
The camouflage only a devil can conceive?
Numbered blocks are renamed with a street sign.
It is paradise here; we are doing fine.
In the park a band shell is erected,
Special lines are taught us and perfected.
"Uncle Rahm,[1] *again we have sardines today?*
We are really sick of them, we want to play."
A children's pavilion set up to impress and show,
Life is normal here; a "fact" for everyone to know.
In the square there is a new café house,
Only the selected are allowed to browse.
We have our own bank and money here,
On which Moses and the tablets appear.
With it nothing but mustard can be bought,
And a new school, in which we are not taught.
Markers to theater and playground,
All will soon be no longer around.
Only special areas are shown with pride,
Most of us are ordered to remain inside.
As fast as commission is out of sight,
We have to bear again tyrannical might.
Soon there will be another selection,
No change; the world believed the deception.

[1] *SS camp commandant.*

Terezin was the antechamber to Auschwitz. Eichmann person-
ally saw to it that there was a constant flow of transports from
Terezin to feed the gas chambers at Auschwitz. He and the SS
commandant of Terezin determined which groups of people were
to be sent East and then ordered the Jewish Council of Elders to

draw up a list of one thousand people from the designated groups for each transport. At one time only old people were called up; at another, the most highly decorated war veterans. The selection process depended entirely on the whims of the SS. We lived day and night with the fear of being sent to the East. There were times when transports left every week. The unfortunate people who had been selected were given a number which was tied around their necks, and were told to assemble at a specific barrack. From there they were forced to enter the cattle cars. The doors were bolted and not opened until their arrival in Auschwitz. Most of the camp Elders eventually suffered the same fate: they, too, were killed in the gas chambers in Auschwitz. When the last selection to the East was made in 1944, all remaining disabled war veterans had to appear at SS headquarters. A red circle was drawn around our names. We had been spared from certain death.

The crematorium at Terezin.

SOMETHING TO REMEMBER ME BY

He was a stranger; we had never met,
He wanted me to recall him, not to forget.
Obviously sensing his awful situation,
Nervous and persuasive in his presentation.

He handed me a box filled with treasure,
And hoped it would give me much pleasure.
Odds and ends up to the brim,
For dreams of any child's whim.
　　　　　"Something to remember me by!"

I was startled and full of surprise,
A rainbow of color before my eyes.
Things made of threads attached to eternity,
Knitted by loving hands without identity.

His eyes looked hopeless; in a daze,
He walked restless, as if in a maze.
He was a humble man—without fame,
Staying unknown—never stating his name.
　　　　　"Something to remember me by!"

He rode away on the death train,
Filled with desperation and pain.
He rests with the ashes in sleep,
His memory I will forever keep.

The little girl now fully grown,
Remembers him, though still unknown.
To this day his words sound loud and clear,
His presence assured from year to year.
　　　　　"Something to remember me by!"

HOLD ME TIGHT

Come with me, my child, hold my hand,
Be calm, my child, do not try to understand.
Don't be afraid, my child, walk with pride,
You know your mother is here at your side.
>   Hold me tight,
>   Day has turned to night,
>   Soon we'll see the light.

No, no, don't look at the chimneys—see the blue sky,
My arm is around you to protect you; don't cry.
Come close—let the blows fall on me,
There'll be a day when again we'll be free.
>   Hold me tight,
>   Day has turned to night,
>   Soon we'll see the light.

Give all your belongings to them, quickly undress,
One day soon we will again have happiness.
Sleep my child—I have no more to give,
Oh, God, Oh, God—we are not going to live!
>   Hold me tight,
>   Day has turned to night,
>   Hold me tight.

My best friend Ruth and her parents, who had shared our bunks
in a tiny room for two years, were in these last transports to the
death camp. She was also an only child, just two months older
than I. We were like sisters and shared our daydreams and se-
crets with each other. She had beautiful blond hair. Her greatest
pleasure was to draw pictures on scraps of paper with colored
pencils that she had smuggled into the camp. She had hopes of
becoming an artist. Ruth and her parents came from Berlin. Her

father walked with a limp caused by a World War I injury. We both found it strange to live with and see around us so many disabled men with missing arms, legs, and other war injuries. Ruth and I owned identical dolls. Before she embarked on her final journey, she entrusted me with all of her doll's clothing, which her mother had carefully sewn from rags. Ruth's father was half Christian and half Jewish, and Ruth was raised as a Christian.

Ruth died because of her Jewish heritage, even though she never considered herself Jewish. She would never live to see her tenth birthday. In "Hold Me Tight," my heart still cries out to her and so many other children as they marched with their mothers to the gas chambers in Auschwitz and the other extermination camps.

CHAPTER 7

✡

Liberation

I learned an old Czech folk song in Terezin. It speaks of the hope and the changes that come with spring. Would we ever be allowed to leave the winter that was Terezin, see the smile of spring, and feel the touch of May again?

Přijde jaro přijde	Spring is in the coming
Bude zase Máj	May is near again
Usmívá se slunce	Sun is warmly smiling
Zelená se háj	Green is meadow's plain
Rozpuknou se ledy	Ice will melt and vanish
Volný bude proud	Streams will freely flow
Po vodach šumících	On silvery waters
Lodě budou plout	Boats will come and go

The spring of 1945 was different from the other two I had spent in Terezin. Unknown to us, Hitler's Third Reich was collapsing and the German armies were facing certain defeat. The Allied forces were closing in on Europe. Meanwhile the Nazis made their last attempts to kill all the remaining survivors in the death camps of the East.

As the Allies advanced, the soldiers forced their prisoners on death marches to places still under complete Nazi rule. I remember when these miserable people arrived at Terezin. They were barefoot, or their feet were covered with rags or torn sandals. Some wore blue and white striped uniforms, others only rags. Their heads were shaved. Many were no more than walking skeletons suffering from typhus and other diseases. In vain I searched the long lines, hoping to find Grandma among them.

During these last days of World War II, orders were given to build gas chambers at Terezin. The plan was to kill us either by poison gas or by drowning in a specially prepared area. Not one Jew in Europe was to stay alive. By the time we were freed, the gas chambers at Terezin were almost completed. It was only the rush of events that spared our lives.

Liberation at Terezin, 1945.

LIBERATION

Guards fearing capture by the Allies began to burn the camp's records. Bits of partially burned paper floated through the air. The evidence of death and suffering had to be destroyed. Then, at the beginning of May, most of the guards living outside the barricades ran away. They made some last efforts to slaughter us as they left, by shooting wildly and throwing hand grenades into the camp.

We were finally liberated on the eve of May 8, 1945 by the Soviet army. The first thing we did was rip off the yellow star from our clothes. I had spent three years in this human hell. I can still see the boisterous Russian soldiers singing and dancing on their tanks. All of us felt joy, pain, and relief. Many questions remained. Who was left of our families? What would our future hold?

After liberation, the barricades were left up for a while, because a severe typhus epidemic was spreading quickly through the camp. Having survived the war, many prisoners died of the disease even after liberation. I remember climbing one of the barricades to accept a piece of black bread with what seemed a mountain of butter from a Russian soldier. I chewed it gently, allowing the butter to melt slowly in my mouth. Was I awake or dreaming?

Despite the typhus quarantine, my father and I went outside the camp walls in search of food. We walked to the fields and picked rhubarb, and in the surrounding towns we begged for food. Back in the camp we bartered the rhubarb for bread and potatoes.

I joined a few other children, and together we stole into the former Nazi living quarters just outside the camp compound. We found bullets lying on the floor and strips of movie film showing sea battles. To our surprise, we saw a swimming pool inside a beautiful park next to these quarters. How different life must have been on the other side of the walls! While we were starving, suffering, and living in fear for our lives, these people just a few yards away lived a life of luxury.

When the typhus epidemic subsided, a few of the survivors began to leave the camp on foot. Most of them did not know where to go or who would help them. Finally, in early July 1945, a bus appeared from Stuttgart, Germany, to pick up the small group of survivors from the state of Württemberg. Out of our original transport of about twelve hundred people, there were thirteen survivors. Three of them were from my family.

LIBERATION

Our camp's population began to swell,
Remnants of other places sent to our hell.
Time was running out; the tyrants began to retreat,
It was clear their armies were facing certain defeat.
One by one each guard was abandoning his post,
The uncertainty what next, we feared the most.
Urgency and anticipation filled the air,
Each minute we were torn between hope and despair.

I climbed the barricade and stole a forbidden glance,
A hand grenade flew close, but missed me by chance.
The sudden explosion gave me a scare,
I touched my head to make sure it was there.
Quickly I sought my parents' side,
In a dark cellar we would hide.
A stream of people joined us as we did descend,
"Could we survive, would this tomb become our end?"
One small candle emitted a ray of light,
A beacon of hope against this darkest might.

Minutes became hours; time was impassively fleeting,
Deadly silence; only the sound of my heart beating.
I found solace in reading my prayer book,
Would someone dare go upstairs and take a look?
Evening had come; the hour was close to nine,
One man chose to go forward and lead the line,
We waited with trepidation; his absence was brief.
"The Allies are here, we are free, we have relief!"

I AM A STAR

MY OMA'S[1] LULLABY

In some strange and distant land,
A life snuffed out by flick of hand.
I hear the shot; I feel the pain,
My Oma did not die in vain.

I read her last postcard now and then,
"With God's help we'll be together again."
Her birthday has become our Yahrzeit[2] date,
To remind us of love and man's hate.

She sang me to sleep with a lullaby,
My child, be happy, do not cry.

Her Shabbos[3] candles had a special glow,
I hope she knew that I loved her so.
Only she held the secret to prepare,
The challes[4] and cakes without compare.

I will always recall her last gaze,
Her eyes, soft smile, and beautiful face.
Her spirit still radiates with undying love,
I know she is looking down at me from above.

She sang me to sleep with a lullaby,
My child, be happy, do not cry.

[1] *Grandma*
[2] *Memorial*
[3] *Sabbath*
[4] *Holiday bread*

We set off from the camp and soon found ourselves passing through badly bombed German cities. The once majestic city of Dresden had been turned completely to rubble. Wherever we stopped, curious Germans gathered outside our bus. One little girl pressed a small doll into my hands and insisted that I keep it and remember her.

After a few days on the road we arrived at the displaced persons' camp in Stuttgart. Here we received our first good meal. I

LIBERATION

remember the beautifully set table and the white tablecloth. I can still taste the noodle soup, which I ate slowly to relish every spoonful. Never in my life would soup taste as good again. We stayed only one week in this temporary facility, which had been especially prepared to house returning Jewish refugees. Our aim was to return to my grandmother's home. We hoped she would still be alive and greet us there.

When we arrived in Jebenhausen, we faced the awful truth. Grandma had not survived. A total of thirteen people from our family had lost their lives during those awful years. Our only hope was to find our beloved Christian friend Therese. To our dismay, the war had claimed her life also. When the American soldiers entered the village, they searched many houses for ammunition. Therese heard the knock on her door, but did not open it, fearing for her life. She remained standing behind the closed door. Eventually, an impatient American soldier shot through the door. She died instantly.

THERESE

To honor her I placed a flower on the grave,
Recalling a woman who generously gave.
Her life in danger; she came in the night,
Bringing food and helping us in our plight.

She did not heed the GI's knock on the door,
A shot rang out; she fell lifeless to the floor.
As before in a distant and strange land,
My grandma's life snuffed out by an SS hand.

I had prayed for their safety every night,
Now they walk together in an unseen light.
The two were inseparable, each a good friend,
A Christian and a Jew united in the end.

71

The new owners of Grandma's house prepared a room for us. When Grandma was deported to Riga in 1941, her house was taken away from us and we were ordered to move into the Jewish houses in Goeppingen. A Christian family received permission to occupy Grandma's house.

Our return after so many years was greeted by a vase filled with field flowers which stood on the table. The Christian family tried to ease our pain. One day someone brought us a big bowl of whipped sweet cream. Mama and I gorged ourselves until we were sick from it. The years of hunger had taken their toll; our stomachs were not ready to digest this rich food.

We soon found more permanent living quarters in the neighboring town of Goeppingen. The mayor invited us to visit him at City Hall. As soon as we stepped into the Mayor's Chamber, Mama noticed the Oriental carpet: it was ours. The mantel clock had a familiar chime; it, too, had once been our property. After our deportation to Terezin, all our belongings had been distributed to different Christian families. Some items had found their way to City Hall.

Inge, parents and an American soldier after liberation, 1945.

LIBERATION

Inge, parents and American soldiers in Goeppingen, 1945.

The townspeople, fearing reprisal from us, insisted that they knew nothing of the horrors we had suffered. They said they had never hated the Jews and were therefore not guilty of any crime. Why then did they not question the fate of so many innocent people taken away so brutally at the time?

Our home became a famililar place for the American soldiers. They showered us with personal goods and candy. Some ran with their melting ice cream rations to our home so that I could have a special treat.

To my knowledge, I was the only Jewish child survivor in the state of Württemberg. My eleventh birthday was a sensation. I was invited to the local UNRRA (United Nations Relief and Rehabilitation Administration) Commission Headquarters. I had but one wish—to receive a new doll carriage, even though I seemed too old for it. I remembered just before my deportation to Terezin how heartbreaking it had been to wheel my light green carriage for two miles to town and give it to another child.

How thrilled I was with my first new outfit, a black and white checked dress sewn especially for me. I felt like an animal let out of a cage. I just wanted to run free and play, instead of studying at school. Papa resumed his textile business and once more began to be successful.

WE HAVE BOTH SURVIVED

As we wandered through the night,
We held on to each other in fright.
Both of us carried on our back,
Few belongings packed in a sack.

While the whips snapped all around,
Only I heard her crying sound.
I held her gently in my arm.
To protect her from any harm.

We both lived through a violent time,
Prisoners, guiltless of any crime.
Even during the greatest despair,
I always knew that she was there.

We calmed and soothed each other,
She was the child, I was the mother.
I felt safe when she was near,
Losing her became my greatest fear.

Now she is brittle, her limbs are worn,
Her clothes are faded with age and torn.
But she still looks at me with loving eyes,
With a warmth that time can't compromise.

She has been carefully stored away,
With memories of many a yesterday.
I thank her for playtime hours spent,
Hoping she knows how much she's meant.

I AM A STAR

Life slowly returned to normal again, but it was still lonely. We took the first opportunity we could to immigrate to America in May 1946. We rode in the boxcars of a freight train to the seaport of Bremen. The cars had been decorated with tree branches, and on their sides was written with chalk: "God bless President Truman and America." It was a stormy ten days at sea on the Marine Perch, an American troop transport ship. We arrived in New York Harbor at night. I stood in awe of the blinking lights of Manhattan, which seemed like a wonderland to me. Lady Liberty was especially bright as her lamp's light welcomed and guided us to a new life. The next morning we disembarked just as the sun rose on a new day.

CHAPTER 8

✡

Afterthoughts

W here were the church and all the good and decent people of the world while this barbarism was going on? The heads of the Christian churches and the leaders of Islam and Buddhism made no protest against this inhumanity. The leaders and intellectuals of the free world did not scream out in protest. Some of the clergy in Belgium and France helped to save Jewish children by hiding them in nunneries and safe houses. Very few of the clergy, however, became involved in this tragedy. Pastor Niemöller of Germany did provide this daring example of the way some people acted during the Nazi era:

> In Germany, the Nazis first came for the Communists, and I didn't speak up because I wasn't a Communist. Then they came for the Jews, and I did not speak up because I was not a Jew. Then they came for the trade unionists, and I didn't speak up because I wasn't a trade unionist. Then they came for the Catholics, and I was a Protestant so I didn't speak up. Then they came for me . . . by that time there was no one to speak up for anyone.

I AM A STAR

Murder on such a scale could not be hidden. The stench of burning flesh from the crematoria reached houses miles away. Many people outside the camps knew of these evil happenings, but did nothing to help. There were some exceptions. The people of Denmark, led by King Christian X, saved seven thousand Jews by helping them escape to Sweden. Raoul Wallenberg, a Swedish diplomat, saved thousands of lives in Hungary. He devised the protective passport, or *Schutzpass*, with the Swedish colors and embassy stamp that placed many Jews in Budapest under Swedish government control. Some of the people of Bulgaria and a few heroic individuals in Germany and the occupied countries risked their lives to aid the Jews.

One might ask, did the Jews go like sheep to slaughter? Yes, they were slaughtered, but not without resistance. Most of them were completely helpless. They had few weapons, were broken in body and spirit; tortured and starved to death. Some were branded like cattle with a tattoo on their left arm. Soap was made from fat of their dead bodies, and human skin was used to make lampshades. Children, especially twins, were used for painful and gruesome medical experiments by Nazi doctors.

There were some heroic acts of resistance by the Jews in the ghettos and camps. One of them was the superhuman effort of the Warsaw Ghetto uprising in April 1943. A small group of poorly armed young Jewish fighters held off the German army for over a month. They did not give up until the Nazis burned the whole ghetto down. Jews were among the first to become partisans (resistance fighters) against the Nazis. There was also resistance of the spirit. Some children in the ghettos and camps were taught against great odds in illegal classes. Just to stay alive one more day was an immense struggle for the human spirit.

What was the toll of these dreadful years? World War II consumed fifty million lives. A total of eleven million people were murdered by starvation, gasing, phenol injection, shooting, electrocution, torture, experimentation, and disease. Six million of them were Jews: two-thirds of the entire Jewish population of Europe had been slaughtered. The other five million humans so

AFTERTHOUGHTS

PEACE

An acorn gives life to a thousand trees,
Many tiny raindrops form the greatest seas.
Nothing is impossible; if only we try,
The smallest tree can reach the sky.

We may differ in thought and ideas,
Every mother cries some salty tears.
If flowers can grow in desert sand,
Hate can turn to love in any land.
> *All wars must cease*
> *There will be peace*

Pick a rose with its thorn,
A world of peace for each newborn.
Let's share the milk and honey today,
Where there is will, there is a way.

Beat each sword into a plowshare,
We must search our hearts and care.
Together we can survive and win,
The time is now; let us begin.
> *All wars must cease*
> *There will be peace*

brutally slain were Gypsies, Slavs, and people who had been branded enemies of the Nazi state. Germany—one of the greatest, most civilized, cultured, and scientifically advanced countries of the world—became the most barbaric nation in history.

Hitler killed himself in his protected bunker in Berlin as the Allies were closing in on him. Some of his aides were tried by an international military tribunal for crimes against humanity. They were sentenced to die or to serve long prison terms. Many escaped to other countries and were never punished for their crimes.

I AM A STAR

The philosopher George Santayana wrote that "those who cannot remember the past are condemned to repeat it." It is our responsibility to be watchful of all our leaders in government. We must speak out against evil and injustice. Let us build bridges of understanding and love to join mankind in every land. My hope, my wish, and prayer is for every child to grow up in peace without hunger and prejudice.

WE SHALL NEVER FORGET

Out of ashes our spirits rise,
Tears rain down from the weeping skies,
We have suffered and endured the fire,
Immense horrors and miles of barbed wire.

History's greatest evil and hell,
We all bear witness, we are here to tell.
The world was deaf, where was the light?
There seemed no end to the long, long night.

CHORUS: *We will always remember, WE SHALL NEVER*
        FORGET!
        Trumpets of joy sound freedom's call,
        Love for God and man, above all,
        WE SHALL NEVER FORGET!

Minds were dulled by bombs of hate,
Only the hero cared about our fate,
We saw the truth, it began to unfold,
You may kill the body but never the soul.

Here we are with honor and pride,
A new generation at our side,
The silent voices join us today,
Never, never again, we hope and pray.

(Repeat CHORUS at will.)

Words by Inge Auerbacher
Music by Rosalie Commentucci

80

Timetable

1919	Adolf Hitler joins the German Workers' Party, which a year later becomes known as the National Socialist German Workers' Party—the Nazi Party.
November 8, 1923	Adolf Hitler leads Beer Hall Putsch in Munich, Germany. He is arrested and sent to jail, where he writes *Mein Kampf.*
January 30, 1933	Adolf Hitler is appointed chancellor of Germany.
March 23, 1933	First concentration camp is established in Dachau, Germany.
April 1, 1933	Boycott of Jewish shops and businesses begins.
April 21, 1933	Ritual slaughter of animals in accordance with Jewish dietary laws is forbidden in Germany.
May 10, 1933	Public burnings of books written by Jews begin.
August 2, 1934	Adolf Hitler is named president and commander-in-chief of the armed forces of Germany.
September 15, 1935	The Nuremberg Laws, anti-Jewish racial laws, come into effect.
March 13, 1938	Austria is added to Germany.
July 6, 1938	Conference to aid political refugees is opened in Evian, France.
September 1938	The Sudetenland, a part of Czechoslovakia, is taken over by Germany.
November 9–10, 1938	On Kristallnacht, or Night of Broken Glass, the anti-Jewish riots erupt in Ger-

	many and Austria. Synagogues are burned, and Jewish houses and businesses are looted and destroyed.
September 1, 1939	Germany invades Poland, and World War II begins.
November 15, 1940	Warsaw Ghetto is sealed off.
March 1941	Adolf Eichmann is appointed head of Gestapo section for Jewish affairs.
September 1, 1941	Jews in Germany must wear the yellow Star of David.
Fall 1941	Auschwitz-Birkenau mass extermination camp in Poland is established. Terezin in Czechoslovakia is selected as a transit camp.
January 20, 1942	Nazis at Wannsee Conference work out plans to murder all the Jews in Europe.
April 19, 1943	Warsaw Ghetto uprising begins.
November 1944	Last Jews are transported from Terezin to Auschwitz.
May 8, 1945	Terezin is liberated by the Soviet army. Germany surrenders to the Allies.

Suggested Further Readings

Altshuler, David A. *Hitler's War against the Jews*. New York: Behrman House, 1978.

Baer, Edith. *A Frost in the Night: A Girlhood on the Eve of the Third Reich*. New York: Pantheon, 1980.

Baldwin, Margaret. *The Boys Who Saved the Children*. New York: Julian Messner, 1981.

Bernbaum, Israel. *My Brother's Keeper—The Holocaust through the Eyes of an Artist*. New York: Putnam, 1985.

Frank, Anne. *Diary of a Young Girl*. New York: Pocket Books (reprint), 1971.

Green, Gerald. *The Artists of Terezin*. New York: Schocken, 1978.

Kantor, Alfred. *The Book of Alfred Kantor*. New York: McGraw-Hill, 1971.

Katz, William Loren. *An Album of Nazism*. New York: Franklin Watts, 1979.

Meltzer, Milton. *Never to Forget*. New York: Harper & Row, 1976.

Orgel, Doris. *The Devil in Vienna*. New York: Dial Press, 1978.

Reiss, Johanna. *The Upstairs Room*. New York: Crowell, 1972.

Richter, Hans Peter. *Friedrich*. New York: Dell, 1973.

Rossel, Seymour. *The Holocaust*. New York: Franklin Watts, 1981.

Rubin, Arnold P. *The Evil That Men Do*. New York: Julian Messner, 1977.

Schoenberner, Gerhard. *The Yellow Star: The Persecution of the Jews in Europe, 1933–1945*. New York: Bantam, 1973.

Volavková, H., ed. *I Never Saw Another Butterfly*. New York: McGraw-Hill, 1964.

Wiesel, Elie. *Night*. New York: Avon, 1972.

Ziemian, Joseph. *The Cigarette Sellers of Three Crosses Square*. New York: Avon, 1977.

Acknowledgments

My most heartfelt thanks go to my beloved parents, who cheered me on and gave me much valuable advice and support in completing my manuscript.

I am immensely grateful to my editor, Denise Johnstone-Burt, whose expert guidance, intellect, talent, and love for humanity are shown in this book.

My most ardent thanks go to Professor Randolph L. Braham, director of the Jack P. Eisner Institute for Holocaust Studies at the City University of New York Graduate Center for sharing his scholarship and for his encouragement. Without his inspiration, friendship, and support this book would never have been written.

I am most grateful to my friend, artist Israel Bernbaum, whose marvelous illustrations express deep emotional feelings and add much value to my book.

I am indebted to editors Iris Rosoff and Diane Arico and to publisher Ron Buehl for believing in me and opening the doors at the Juvenile Division of Simon & Schuster.

I would like to express my sincere thanks to my dear friends Else Bakke, Orest Dutka, and Mollie Kramer of the Jackson Heights Branch of the Queens Borough Public Library, who helped me so much in spirit and research in completing this book.

My special appreciation is extended to Elenore Lester, associate editor of *The Jewish Week*, for her friendship and emotional support.

Many thanks go to authors Judy Blume and Herman Wouk for lending a helping hand.

I am deeply grateful for and will never forget the help given me by Art Raymond, of radio station WEVD-FM, who was the first to bring my writing to the attention of a large audience.

My thanks go to composers Rosalie Commentucci-O'Hara, with whom my dream began, and to Barney Bragin, James Donenfeld, and Sol Zim, who added so much talent to my words.

I acknowledge the support given me by my boss, Dr. Rolf Zilversmit, and my co-workers Ruth R. Goldberg and Vivian Hershfield, who gave me much advice and encouragement in writing my book. I greatly appreciate their understanding of my situation during the stressful time of writing.

I am grateful for the permission to reproduce photographs from the Kulturamt-Stadtarchiv, Landeshauptstadt Stuttgart, State Jewish Museum in Prague and the YIVO Institute For Jewish Research.

Appreciation goes to Dr. Karel Jindrak for his English translation of the Czech folk song: "Spring is in the Coming."

I would like to thank the following for their help in my research: Dan Weissman, Prof. Henry Huttenbach, Rabbi Herman Dicker, Dr. Kurt Maier, The Simon Wiesenthal Center, Center For Holocaust Studies, Inc., the Anti-Defamation League of B'nai B'rith and the American Jewish Committee.

I am thankful to many people, too numerous to mention, whose omission is no measure of the help they gave me in achieving an important point in my life.

About the Author

Inge Auerbacher was born in Kippenheim, Germany. She was imprisoned from 1942 to 1945 in the Terezin concentration camp in Czechoslovakia when she was seven to ten years of age. In 1946 she immigrated to the United States of America and has lived since then in New York City.

She graduated from Queens College with a B.S. degree in chemistry and has done postgraduate work in biochemistry at Hunter College. She has been associated with many renowned researchers in the field of medicine. Today she is in charge of the coagulation laboratory for Mount Sinai Services at City Hospital Center in Elmhurst.

Ms. Auerbacher is a world traveler, travel writer, and avid photographer. More than fifty of her poems on various themes have been published. She wrote the lyrics for "We Shall Never Forget," the only original song presented at the World Gathering of Jewish Holocaust Survivors, 1981 in Jerusalem. The lyrics are set to music written by Rosalie Commentucci-O'Hara. The record album, *Jewish Memories*, contains four of Ms. Auerbacher's lyrics, sung by the cantor and entertainer Sol Zim. Other lyrics have been set to music by James Donenfeld and Barney Bragin.

Inge Auerbacher appeared in *Childhood Memories of the Holocaust*, a television documentary produced in 1985 by the New York City Board of Education. She spends much of her free time lecturing on the Holocaust.